COUNTRY TOPICS

JAPAN

RICHARD AND SHEILA TAMES

Illustrated by Teri Gower

FRANKLIN WATTS
NEW YORK • CHICAGO • LONDON • TORONTO • SYDNEY

This symbol appears on some pages throughout this book. It indicates that adult supervision is advisable for that activity.

Library of Congress Cataloguing-in-Publication Data
Tames, Richard.
Japan/Richard and Sheila Tames.
p. cm. -- (Country Topics for craft projects)
Includes index.
ISBN 0-531-14315-5
1. Japan--Juvenile literature.   [1. Japan.]
I. Tames, Sheila. II. Title. III. Series.
DS806.T292   1994
952--dc20   93-42886
                                     CIP
                                       AC

Paperback edition published in 1995
ISBN 0-531-15277-4

Franklin Watts
A Division of Grolier Publishing
Sherman Turnpike
Danbury, CT 06816

Editor: Hazel Poole
Designer: Sally Boothroyd
Photography: Peter Millard
Artwork: Teri Gower
Picture Research: Veneta Bullen

Printed in the United Kingdom

CONTENTS

Introducing Japan

YOKOSO!
Welcome!
Glad to see you!
Before you start
to explore, here
are a few useful
facts about Japan.

FLYING THE FLAG

The Japanese flag is called *Hinomaru,* which means "circle of the sun." It has a red circle on a white background. The red circle represents the sun because the emperors of Japan used to claim to be descended from Amaterasu Omikami – the Sun Goddess. In the traditional religion of Japan, Shinto, white represents purity.

JAPAN IN THE WORLD

Japan consists of a chain of islands off the eastern coast of Asia, covering an area of 145,280 square miles (377,727 sq km). Its capital is Tokyo – which means "Eastern Capital." As you can see from the map, Japan's nearest neighbors are Russia, Korea, and China. Although Russia has occupied the Kuril Islands since 1945, Japan claims them as Japanese territory. Japan is situated 124 miles (200 km) from Korea and 466 miles (750 km) away from China.

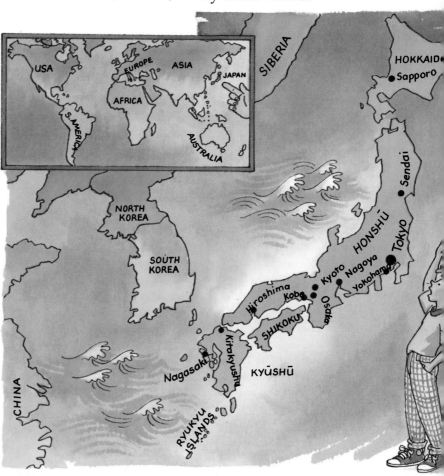

Japan is a democratic monarchy. Its name in Japanese is *Nippon.* The head of state is the emperor. His duties are ceremonial, such as presenting national awards. The prime minister leads the government. The National Diet (parliament) is made up of the House of Representatives and the House of Councillors.

KIMIGAYO

The Japanese national anthem is called *Kimigayo*, which means "His Majesty's Reign." The words come from a poem written over one thousand years ago and wishes the emperor a happy reign of thousands of years. It was first set to music in 1880 and is sung in schools and before sports events. But no law has ever been passed to make it the official anthem.

JAPANESE MONEY

The Japanese currency is called the *yen*, written as ¥. You can get bills for the following amounts – 500, 1,000, 5,000, and 10,000, and there are coins for 1, 5, 10, 50, 100, and 500 yen. Personal checks are rarely used, though plastic credit cards are becoming more common. Most people are used to carrying around large sums of cash. This is quite safe as robbery is rare in Japan.

KEEP TO THE LEFT

In Japan you drive on the left-hand side of the road, so cars have their steering wheels on the right. Traffic tends to move rather slowly as the roads are very crowded, and in the cities they are very narrow. Often there are no pavements, although pedestrians are protected by barriers on side streets. Parking is also a big problem. Many people use bicycles, and public transportation is very efficient.

Say it in Japanese
hata – flag
kitte – stamp
okane – money
Nippon – Japan
Nihonjin – Japanese person
chizu – map

Saying It in Japanese

THE EASY PART

Japanese grammar and the Japanese system of writing are both difficult, but pronouncing Japanese is not. These are some of the main rules:

1. Each syllable in every word is stressed evenly.
2. Each syllable ends in a vowel, except when *n* comes at the end of a word.
3. Sometimes vowels are skipped over or ignored. For example, the name *Matsushita* is pronounced *Matsush'ta*, and the word *desu* (meaning "is" or "are") is pronounced *dess*.
4. Where two consonants come together, they are both pronounced. For example, *kekko* ("enough") is pronounced as *kek-ko*.

THE HARD PART

Japanese is written with three kinds of script. There are two syllabaries called *kana*, each of which has forty-eight symbols. The kana are like alphabets, but whereas an alphabet is made up of single letters, a syllabary is made up of symbols that stand for the sound of complete syllables.

The *hiragana* syllabary has curved symbols, and the *katakana* has angular ones. Words and names taken from foreign languages are usually written in katakana.

The third kind of script consists of Chinese characters, known as *kanji*. These were originally pictures of things but they were gradually made simpler until they became like diagrams. It is not possible to tell how a character should be pronounced just by looking at it. Kanji can be combined to make new words. You have to know at least 1,800 kanji to be able to read a newspaper!

Here are some names written in kana:

Ann アン   John ジョン

Try using the kana chart to write your own name.

Here are some common kanji and some pictures to show what they were like originally:

Fire 火   Mountain 山

River 川   Tree 木

NAMES

Japanese put their family name before their first name, and they only use first names with very close friends. They usually use the family name with *san* added to the end, which means Mr., or Mrs., or Ms.

Many Japanese family names refer to places or nature. *Yamamura* means "mountain village" and *Tachibana* means "orange tree."

Here are some common Japanese family names:		
Ito	Watanabe	Tanaka
Sato	Kobayashi	Nakamura

Here are some common girls' names:		
Akiko	Yuko	Toshiko
Keiko	Mariko	Mitsuko

Here are some common boys' names:		
Yoshio	Hiroshi	Ichiro
Yukio	Kenzo	Akira

Sun 日

Mouth 口

BEING POLITE

Japanese are very polite. When people meet for the first time, they exchange name cards. A name card usually says what job a person does. This helps people to judge how politely they should speak to the other person.

There are special phrases for many everyday occasions. Before eating, you should say *itadakimasu* (pronounced itta-dakky-mass). This means "I receive." Afterward you should say *gochisosama deshita* (pronounced go-chee-so-samma-deshta), which means "Everything was delicious."

Say it in Japanese
Watashiwa Ann desu – I am Ann
ohayogozaimasu – good morning
konnichiwa – good day
kombanwa – good evening
oyasumi nasai – good night
sayonara – goodbye
Ogenki desuka? – How are you?
Hai, genkidesu – Yes, fine

Around Japan

From north to south, Japan is as long as America from Maine to Florida and has an even more extreme range of climate. Natural disasters and war have destroyed many historic landmarks, but the ancient buildings that survive attract millions of visitors.

Average temperatures

Place	Winter	Summer
Kyushu	45°F (7°C)	81°F (27°C)
Hokkaido	16°F (–9°C)	70°F (21°C)

JAPANESE GEOGRAPHY

Japan is a country of cities, mountains, and islands. This map shows the names of the most important ones as well as some of the famous places that attract visitors.

The weather in southern Japan is humid in summer. In the north, the winters are long and snowy. The Japan Sea coast has colder, wetter weather than the Pacific coast. In the autumn, southern Japan often suffers from typhoons. Earthquakes and tidal waves are less frequent but more damaging. The earthquake and tidal wave that hit west of Hokkaido in 1993 killed almost 100 people.

Japan has one-tenth of the world's active volcanoes, including Mount Aso, the largest. The island of Kyushu is famous for its springs of hot water and mud.

DIALECTS

At school all Japanese children are taught a standard form of their language, which is also used in broadcasting. There are strong local accents and differences of vocabulary in the way Japanese is spoken in the Tohoku region of northern Honshu, around Osaka, and on the island of Okinawa.

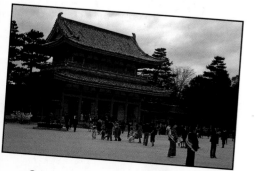

SHINJUKU

Tokyo has only had tall skyscrapers since the 1960s. They have to be earthquake-proof and most of them are near Shinjuku, the city's busiest station. Over one million people pass through it every day. Tokyo Tower, completed in 1958, stands in nearby Shiba Park. At 1,092 feet (333 m), it is 10 percent higher than the Eiffel Tower in Paris.

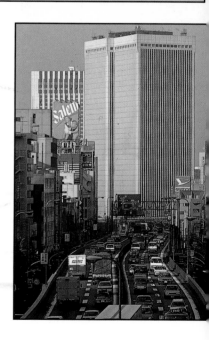

KYOTO

Kyoto was the capital of Japan for almost nine hundred years. It still has hundreds of old shrines, temples, and gardens. It is famous for traditional crafts such as silk weaving, pottery, and lacquerware. More than twenty million visitors come to Kyoto every year.

MOUNT FUJI

Many artists and poets have been inspired by the beauty of Mount Fuji. As Japan's highest mountain, it stands at 12,389 feet (3,776 m). On a clear day it can be seen from 93 miles (150 km) away. It can only be climbed in July and August, and each year half a million people climb it. Mount Fuji is a volcano which last erupted in 1707.

POLLUTION

The Japanese have become very aware of the problem of pollution. In big cities, screens show the public the level of pollution in the air as it changes.

Say it in Japanese

natsu – summer
fuyu – winter
taiyo – sun
ame – rain
onsen – hot spring
kisha – train
kawa – river
yama – mountain

BULLET TRAIN

Japan's famous "bullet train" service was started in 1964. It covers the 345 miles (555 km) between Tokyo and Osaka in 3 hours and 10 minutes. At peak times, up to 100 bullet trains are in service, each with 16 cars. They are extremely punctual and safe.

Food and Drink

Japanese restaurants are now becoming popular in other countries, especially in the United States. The Japanese diet is very healthy because it has very little fat in it. A normal meal, including breakfast, will consist of boiled rice, fish, and vegetables, cooked, raw, or pickled.

Over the last fifty years, Japanese people have begun to eat more Western foods such as cheese, beef, and bread.

SHOPPING FOR FOOD

Japanese people insist on having their fish and vegetables as fresh as possible. This is because both are often eaten raw. Most housewives go shopping every day. Local shops deliver heavy things, such as bags of rice or cases of beer, to the customer's home.

Shopping list
kome - rice
sakana - fish
shoyu - soy sauce
o-cha - tea
kohii - coffee
yasai - vegetables

DRINKS

Green tea, without milk or sugar, is served with every meal. The traditional alcoholic drink is *sake*, a clear drink made from rice. It is drunk warmed in winter and chilled in summer. Today lager-type beer and whisky are as popular. A sweet-flavored sake, called *mirin*, is used in cooking.

Japanese restaurants often specialize in a particular type of dish:

TEMPURA consists of pieces of fish, shrimp, or vegetable, fried very quickly in a light batter to make a crisp, crunchy mouthful. Tempura dishes must be eaten immediately.

YAKITORI is a sort of Japanese kebab consisting of pieces of richly flavored chicken grilled on a skewer.

SUSHI are patties of vinegared rice, topped with different kinds of fish, or rolled around pickles.

SASHIMI is raw fish which is cut into bite-size chunks, dipped in a sauce, and then eaten.

JAPANESE COOKING

Traditional Japanese kitchens had no oven, so baking and roasting were unknown. The normal cooking methods were grilling, frying, or boiling.

Japanese cooks take the greatest possible care in presenting food. Special attention is paid to choosing bowls of the right color and shape.

Soy beans are an essential ingredient for Japanese cooking. They are fermented to make salty soy sauce or made into a paste, called *miso*, which is used for flavoring or thickening soups and stews. Soy beans are also made into a curd (a bit like cheese) called *tofu*. It is rich in protein and vitamins but low in calories.

EATING OUT

Japanese people do not usually take long over lunch. A bowl of hot noodles is cheap and filling. Travelers can buy attractive boxed lunches at railroad stations. Businessmen often entertain customers at restaurants in the evening. Before a meal is served, cutomers are each given a steaming-hot towel to wipe their hands with. Housewives meet their friends at coffee shops during the day. In the spring, families often go out to have a picnic in the countryside.

CHOPSTICKS

When they eat at home, Japanese people use lacquered or plastic chopsticks which are washed afterward. When they eat out, Japanese people use wooden chopsticks which are thrown away afterward. Cooks use very long chopsticks instead of tongs or a whisk when preparing food.

Say it in Japanese
mizu – water
resutoran – restaurant
bento – boxed lunch
oishii – delicious
sarada – salad
hanbaga – hamburger
jusu – soft drink

11

A Taste of Japan

Ebi to yasai no iri-tamago means scrambled egg with shrimp and vegetables!

This dish is light, tasty, and easy to make, and the recipe below should be enough for two servings.

YOU WILL NEED:

1 nonstick pan
1 small saucepan
1 spatula
bowls
hot water
4 mushrooms (diced)
4 eggs
20 small shrimp (peeled)
salt & pepper
2 tablespoons salad oil
3 tablespoons soy sauce
4 tablespoons frozen peas
1 tablespoon sugar
1 chicken stock cube, dissolved in 1¾ cups hot water

1. Soak the shrimp and the frozen peas in some hot water to defrost them. When defrosted, drain, and set aside for a few moments.

2. In a small saucepan, combine the soy sauce, sugar, and 1/2 cup of chicken stock. Heat gently until the sugar dissolves.

3. Add shrimp, peas, and diced mushrooms to the saucepan and cook gently for 5 minutes. Drain into a dish, and put the liquid to one side.

4. Break the eggs into a bowl and beat thoroughly. Season with a little pepper. Add 3 tablespoons of the sauce to the eggs. Mix well.

5. Heat the salad oil in a pan over medium heat. Add the egg mixture and stir well. As the mixture begins to cook, add the shrimp, peas, and mushrooms. Keep stirring until the mixture is nearly set but still looks quite creamy. Serve immediately in a small bowl.

Try eating it with chopsticks! It's okay to lift the bowl up and hold it near your mouth.

Radish Flowers

In Japan rice, fish, pickles and so on are served in separate bowls and dishes. This is a simple way of preparing radishes to make an attractive side-dish.

YOU WILL NEED:

2 tablespoons wine vinegar or cider vinegar

chopping board

sharp kitchen knife

I cup of water

6 radishes

bowl

1. Clean the radishes well, but do not scrub the skins too hard.

2. Hold each radish firmly with the top pointing upwards. Make a cut across the top pressing the knife down until it is nearly halfway in. Make another cut close to the first one and continue cutting across the top.

3. Now make the same sort of cut at right angles to the first ones so that it looks like this.

4. When you have cut all the radishes, put them into a bowl with the water and vinegar and let them soak for a couple of hours. Gradually they will open out into "flowers" and the water will turn pink.

Fun with paper

Folding a piece of paper into a beautiful shape is called *origami*. The art of origami began in Japan at least three hundred years ago. Food is sometimes served on paper folded into interesting shapes. Also, paper shapes are used to decorate tables.

Here is a fun and simple helmet (*boshi*) shape to make.

a square piece of paper

1. Place the paper in a diamond shape.

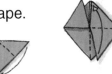

3. Fold the points up and out like this.

2. Fold bottom edge up and top corner along the middle. Fold points down again.

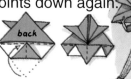

back

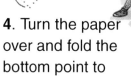

4. Turn the paper over and fold the bottom point to the middle.

5. Finally turn it back and fold the narrow point like this.

Life in Japan

WHERE PEOPLE LIVE

Most Japanese people live in very large cities. Japan has eleven cities that each have a population of more than one million, and another ten cities that each have more than half a million people living in them. Many people have to travel an hour or more to get to work. Homes are cramped by Western standards and few have gardens. Houses are built of lightweight materials and are usually rebuilt about every thirty years.

Country areas tend to have less young people living in them as they move to the cities for work. But even people who have lived in cities for generations, remember their family's home village and go back there for festivals.

In Japan people usually sleep on futons. Here you can see lots of futons being dried and aired.

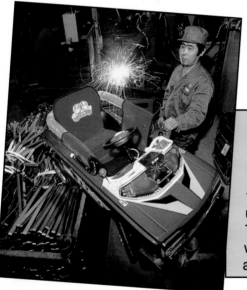

In some factories, robots perform tasks that people used to do. This toy car was built by a robot.

WHAT PEOPLE DO

Today more people work in shops and offices than in factories or on the land. Japan's millions of small businesses employ far more people than the few big companies who are known worldwide. The fastest growing industries are electronics, computers, and robotics. More and more women and older people are working, especially in part-time jobs.

POLICE

Japan is a very law-abiding country with a low crime rate. In the cities there are lots of police kiosks to be found. Policemen know their neighborhoods well and visit every home regularly.

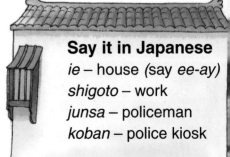

Say it in Japanese
ie – house *(say ee-ay)*
shigoto – work
junsa – policeman
koban – police kiosk

14

GOING TO SCHOOL

Japanese children must go to school from the age of six to fifteen. Most go to a preschool group before they are six, and stay in school until they are eighteen. About 40 percent then go on to college. Pupils go to school for 192 days of the year and have homework over summer vacation, too. Standards are very high, and almost all Japanese children study English.

Junior School (1st Years : age 12/13)							
Subject	Mon	Tues	Wed	Thurs	Fri	Sat	Sun
8.30 – 8.40			FORM	TIME			
8.45 – 9.35	Math	Japanese	P.E.	Social Studies	English	Music	
9.45 – 10.35	Japanese	English	Science	Japanese	Art	Math	
10.45 – 11.35	Social Studies	Calligraphy	Japanese	P.E.	Art	P.E.	
11.35 – 12.35			LUNCH	TIME			
12.35 – 1.25	Music	Science	Math	English			
1.35 – 2.25	Science	Social Studies	Moral Studies	Form Discussion			

KEEPING INFORMED

The three main daily newspapers are the *Asahi*, *Mainichi*, and *Yomiuri*. In the Tokyo area there are also seven television channels to choose from. Comic books are very popular and are read by adults as well as children.

SHOPS ON EVERY CORNER

In Japan you can find lots of big department stores, usually with their own restaurant and art gallery. There are even more small corner shops, which often stay open very late in the evenings. Most big shops are usually open on Sundays.

Say it in Japanese
gakko – school
sensei – teacher
shimbun – newspaper
terebi – television
manga – comic book
kaimono – shopping
depato – department store

Sport

The Japanese take sports very seriously. They have lessons, read books about it, and get all the right equipment. Because land is scarce, sports that need large areas of grass, such as golf, are expensive. Indoor sports and hard court sports, like tennis or volleyball, are cheaper and more popular.

GOLF

It costs a lot to build a golf course in Japan, and players have to pay very high fees. Most Japanese have to make do with practicing at a driving range.

MARTIAL ARTS

Martial arts began as a way for samurai warriors to keep in training during times of peace.

Judo is a form of unarmed self-defense. The main aim is to use an opponent's own strength to throw him off balance. The word judo means "way of gentleness."

Karate means "empty hand." When the people of Okinawa had their weapons taken from them, they developed karate as a means of defense.

Kendo is Japanese-style fencing. Fencers wear body armor, gauntlets, and a face mask. The springy "swords" are made of bamboo.

BASEBALL

Baseball is Japan's most popular spectator sport. Professional teams are sponsored by department stores, newspapers, and food companies. The highlight of the baseball year is the final of the national competition between high schools.

SOCCER

Soccer is Japan's newest craze. A professional league was started in 1993. Famous foreign players were brought in to make the sport popular. One of these was Gary Lineker, the former English soccer captain.

Say it in Japanese
budo – martial arts
yakyu – baseball
sakka – soccer
tenisu – tennis
gorufu – golf

SUMO

Sumo wrestling has been a professional sport for 200 years. The wrestlers eat a special diet to get big. Many weigh as much as 400 pounds. Sumo bouts take place in a circle made by a straw rope. The winner is the one who forces his opponent out of the circle or makes him touch the floor with any part of his body other than his feet. Sumo tournaments last 10 days and are held six times a year. The winners get the title of *yokozuma* – "grand champion."

Leisure

LOCAL FESTIVALS

There are thousands of local festivals. They began when most people were farmers. In the spring, they held a festival to ask the gods to look after the crops they were planting. In the autumn, they would give thanks for the harvest. Festivals may involve parades, dances, feasts, or even contests such as tug-of-war, horse races, or kite flying.

During the time of the Star Festival *"Tanabata"*, people take to the streets to celebrate.

NEW YEAR

The most important celebration is the New Year. On New Year's Day most families go to a shrine to pray for good health and prosperity in the coming year. Food is prepared in advance and eaten cold so that the cook can join in the celebrations. New Year's cards are sent out from mid-December onward, but deliberately held by the post office so that they can all be delivered on New Year's Day by an army of students specially hired for the job.

GOLDEN WEEK

There are three national holidays that fall very close together – Environment Day (April 29), Constitution Day (May 3), and Children's Day (May 5). Most people take off the days in between to give them a week-long break.

Swim for it

HOLIDAYS

Japanese people do not usually take long vacations. It is more usual to take a trip for two or three days. Favorite destinations include the beaches, mountains, hot springs, or an ancient city, like Kyoto. Skiing trips are also popular in winter.

AGE FESTIVALS

January 15 is "Coming of Age" Day. People who have reached the age of twenty in the past year can now vote, and are all invited to the local town hall.

On Children's Day (May 5), carp streamers are displayed. This fish swims against the stream and is thought to be a good example of strength and determination.

Shichigosan (seven-five-three) falls on November 15. Girls aged three or seven, and boys aged three or five, go to give thanks at a temple for growing up healthy. The girls wear a silk kimono and have their hair dressed with combs and pins.

December 23 is celebrated because it is the birthday of the emperor.

Say it in Japanese
saijitsu – national holiday
matsuri – festival
Shogatsu – New Year
tanjobi – birthday

HOW TO MAKE AND DECORATE A CARP STREAMER

YOU WILL NEED:

brushes and paints
acrylic glue
small piece of silver paper
scissors
pencil
smaller sheets of colored paper
1 large piece of thick paper 40 ins X 16 ins

1. Fold the large piece of paper in half lengthwise.

2. Draw the outline of half a fish.

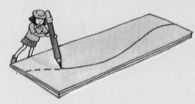

3. Cut around the outline, and then unfold the paper. You should have a symmetrical fish.

4. Cut out some fins from darker paper. You need one top fin and two lower fins. Glue them onto your fish and add some stripes. Paint the tail fin to match.

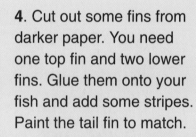

5. For the scales, cut out lots of fan shapes from the colored paper. Paint the curved edge with dark paint.

6. Stick the scales onto your fish in overlapping rows. Then add an eye made from silver foil.

Japanese Style

KIMONO

The traditional Japanese kimono is a one-size garment. In the past, kimonos for everyday wear were made out of cotton or linen. Today synthetic materials are used as well. Kimonos for special occasions were made of silk and dyed or embroidered with decorations. Young girls wore bright colors and big patterns. Older women wore dark colors and small patterns. The long sleeves were used as pockets. When housewives were working, they tied the sleeves behind their backs. Today most people only wear kimonos on special occasions such as weddings or at New Year's.

FUROSHIKI

The furoshiki is a square of cloth used for carrying things in a bundle. Originally furoshiki were used by people to wrap their clothes in when they went to the public bathhouse. Furoshiki usually have a striking pattern embroidered or dyed on them. Modern fashion designers have used them to make into blouses or vests.

WESTERN CLOTHES

Japanese began wearing Western-style clothes over 100 years ago, but they have only become common outside cities since 1945. Japanese men usually wear plain, dark suits to the office. Japanese women are very fashion conscious and spend a lot of money on clothes and makeup.

YUKATA

The *yukata* is an unlined, white cotton kimono, with a blue pattern. It is worn by both men and women and used as a bathrobe or instead of pajamas. It is very comfortable to wear at home on warm summer evenings.

GETA

These are wooden clogs which used to be worn because the old Japanese roads were very muddy. They were left outside the house, and even today, Japanese people never wear shoes inside their homes.

DESIGN A HAPPI COAT

A happi coat is a short, loose jacket worn in Japan by people at work, such as gardeners, shopkeepers, firemen, craftsmen, or fishermen. They are often brightly colored or have bold, simple designs. Some carry advertisements such as the name of a shop or business. They are tied around the waist with a contrasting band of cloth.

Happi coats are also worn at festivals. The example shown below has two *torii* on the front. A torii is a gateway that marks the entrance to a Shinto shrine. The design on the back shows three arrows. Many shrines sell toy arrows with "fortunes" printed on them.

Why not design your own version?

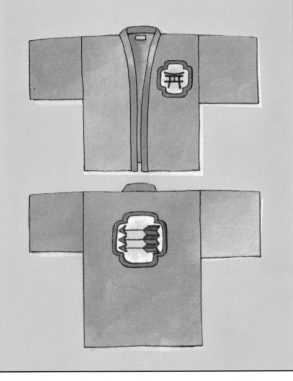

A KIMONO DOLL BOOKMARK

gift wrap paper

tape

scissors

ribbon

stiff cardboard

YOU WILL NEED:

1. Copy this shape onto some stiff cardboard and cut it out. Paint on a face and some hair.

2. Cut your giftwrap paper into a rectangle as tall as the doll, and three times as wide. Make a 3/8 inch (1 cm) fold along one of the long edges. Place the figure in the middle of the plain side of the paper.

3. Wrap both sides of the paper across the front of your doll. Fold the overlapping edges around the back and glue them down.

4. Make a sash from a contrasting piece of paper and attach it at the back with tape.

5. Cut a thin strip of ribbon and place it over the sash. Attach this at the back with tape, too.

Why not try making your own decorated paper and make more dolls in the same way?

The Arts

Modern Japan has its own world-class musicians, writers, and artists. In the past, Japan developed some very special arts all of its own.

CALLIGRAPHY

Writing used to be done using a brush. Poems were written on scrolls of fine paper and hung up on the wall. The Japanese still admire calligraphy, the art of writing beautifully. At New Year's many schools hold calligraphy competitions.

TEA CEREMONY

Tea was introduced from China. At first it was used as a medicine. Then monks began to drink it to keep awake during the long hours of prayer and meditation. Serving tea in calm surroundings became a way of soothing people's problems. A full-length tea ceremony can last up to four hours. In one version, the guest will eat a sweet, sip the tea, and then admire the beauty of the cup. Many Japanese girls are still taught how to perform this ceremony properly.

ARCHITECTURE

Japanese builders like to use the natural textures of wood, bamboo, and paper for their decorative effect.

KABUKI

This is a kind of theater with very dramatic makeup and costumes. The heroes are often samurai. Even the women's parts are played by men. There are lots of special tricks, such as revolving stages and trapdoors that make the actors disappear.

There are two other kinds of drama – *noh*, where the actors wear masks, and *bunraku*, in which the actors manipulate puppets two-thirds life size.

WOODBLOCK PRINTS

The Japanese invented color printing around 1750, much earlier than in Europe. The prints were quite cheap and used to advertise plays or to make souvenirs showing famous places.

FLOWER ARRANGEMENT

This art began with placing offerings of flowers in front of statues of Buddha. Most girls take lessons in flower arranging. Arrangements are found in most offices and homes. The Japanese also like to grow miniature trees (*bonsai*).

Say it in Japanese
shodo – calligraphy
ikebana – flower arranging
chado – tea ceremony

23

Tabletop Gardening

The Japanese love gardens. Garden designers are regarded as artists, just like painters or sculptors. In Japanese gardens trees, shrubs, stones, gravel, and water are usually more important than flowers. Many gardens are miniature versions of a landscape with mountain ranges, rivers, and cliffs. Some temple gardens consist of raked sand and rocks without any plants at all. Often trees and shrubs are closely clipped to make interesting shapes.

Because most Japanese live in crowded cities, very few people have a big garden of their own. Some people make miniature gardens in trays.

YOU WILL NEED:

a metal tray with a raised edge

thin cardboard

a piece of thick cardboard larger than the tray

a comb with big teeth

stones

small mirror

modeling knife

acrylic glue

drinking straws

fine sand

paper towels

modeling clay

small twigs, ferns, leaves

paints and brushes

toothpicks

1. Cut the cardboard so that it fits inside the tray. A dab of glue should keep it in place.

2. Decide where you want to put your lake (mirror) and stick it in position. You can make it an interesting or unusual shape by sticking a "frame" made from thin cardboard over it.

3. Now decide which parts of your garden are going to be gravel. Spread a thin layer of glue over these areas and lightly sprinkle the fine sand on top. When it has dried, you can add some more, and then rake it into patterns with the comb.

4. Arrange your rocks. The big ones might stand alone, and the smaller ones in groups. You could put some across the lake as stepping stones.

5. Fill in your areas of greenery using ferns and leaves. You may need to stand them in lumps of modeling clay to support them. Paint some paper towels green and use this as close-cut grass.

6. Glue some paper towels around some drinking straws. Paint them yellow-brown to look like bamboo. You can also use toothpicks to make a bamboo fence.

7. You might like to put a wall around your garden. Paint some thick cardboard dark gray to look like stone.

Instant Poetry

The very first books ever written in Japanese were collections of legends and poems. Emperors liked writing poetry. Even today the emperor holds a poem-writing competition every year.

The most famous kind of Japanese poem is the *haiku* It is a very short poem with only three lines. A haiku poem is too short to tell a story, and it is usually about nature and the changing seasons of the year. Small creatures, such as flies or mice, are often the subjects of haiku.

Try writing your own haiku, bearing in mind that the middle line should be longer than the other two.

Why not write about one of the following:

the seashore
a sparrow
a waterfall
a snake

Remember that haiku usually refer to events taking place in a particular season of the year. A waterfall would be very different at the end of winter compared to the end of mid-summer.

Haiku has been translated into English and French since around 1900. Poets now write haiku in those languages.

The most famous haiku poe was Basho (1644–1694).

His best-known poem goes like this in Japanese:

*Furuike ya
Kawazu tobikomu
Mizu no oto.*

A literal translation might be

*The old pond
A frog jumps in
Sound of water.*

A more poetic version might be:

*The cloudy waters
Call the frog to deep beneath
Splash!– he's just vanished!*

YOU WILL NEED:

3 strips of colored
paper of different
sizes

short
length
of bamboo

acrylic glue

thick cotton or thin
ribbon

felt-tip pens
or brush and
ink

At the time of the Star
Festival (*Tanabata*) on July 7,
some families buy a bamboo branch
and decorate it with poems or wishes
written on strips of decorated paper.
Perhaps originally the idea was that the wind
would carry the wishes to the gods so that they
could help them come true.

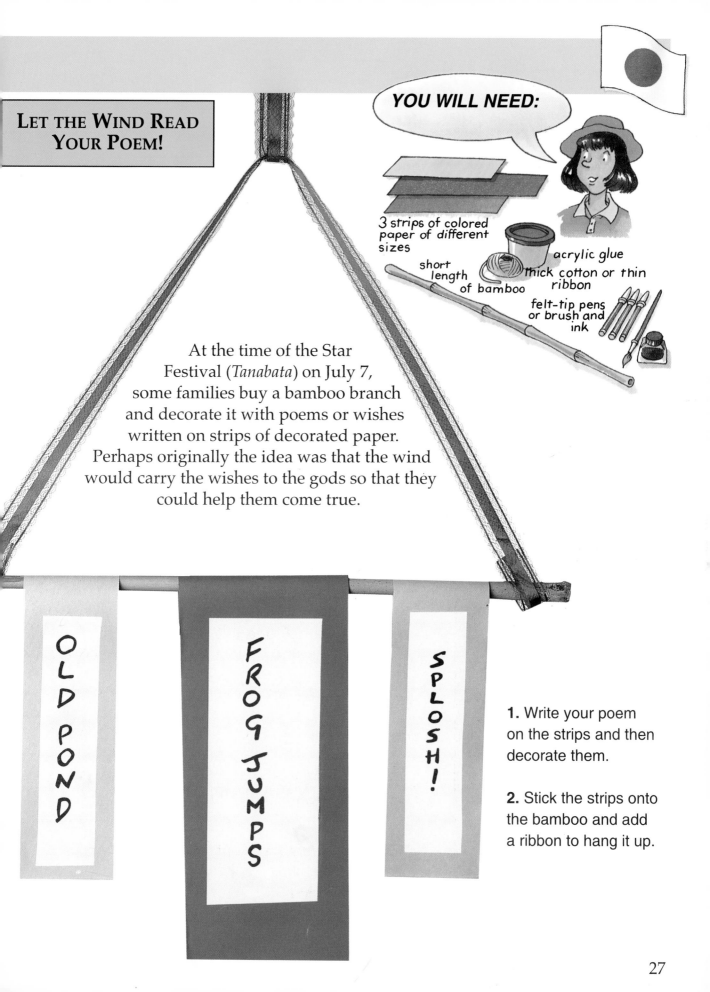

OLD POND

FROG JUMPS

SPLOSH!

1. Write your poem
on the strips and then
decorate them.

2. Stick the strips onto
the bamboo and add
a ribbon to hang it up.

Japanese History

Japan is an old country with a long and dramatic history. Here are some of the key events and characters.

NEW IDEAS FROM CHINA

Chinese and Korean visitors introduced writing and the Buddhist religion. Buddhism had a great effect on Japanese art. Japanese also learned how to make silk, lacquer, and fine pottery. A planned, permanent capital was built, first at Nara, and then at Kyoto.

THE SAMURAI

Samurai warriors fought for power. The winner was called the shogun and he claimed to rule on behalf of the emperor. Samurai were trained to be fearless. They would sooner kill themselves than surrender in battle. Many Japanese towns grew up around the castles built for the samurai. The samurai always wore two swords, a big one for fighting with and a smaller one for cutting off an enemy's head or killing himself with if he thought he might be captured and beaten.

WILLIAM ADAMS

William Adams was shipwrecked in Japan in 1600 and was the first Englishman to set foot there. He became a friend of the shogun and built Western-style ships for him. In return, the shogun made Adams a samurai. This was the only time that this title was given to somebody who was not Japanese. Adams helped English ships trade with Japan, but he never returned to England.

JAPAN MODERNIZES

In 1868, a group of young samurai seized power in the name of Emperor Meiji. They brought in Western experts to build railroads and factories and train a modern army and navy. Japan began to be an important trading nation. Through wars against China and Russia, Japan built up an overseas empire.

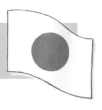

EARTHQUAKE!

In 1923, a terrible earthquake hit Tokyo and Yokohama. It happened at noon when fires were lit in most homes to cook lunch. Most houses were made of wood so there were huge fires. About 140,000 people died. It was Japan's worst earthquake in modern times.

Say it in Japanese
rekushi – history
ten-no – emperor
shogun – warlord

TOKYO OLYMPICS

In 1964, the Olympic Games were held in Japan. A new "Bullet Train" service was started to carry visitors between the two main cities where the Games were held – Tokyo and Kyoto. The Bullet Train goes at 124 miles per hour (200 km/h). In 1972, the Winter Olympics were held at Sapporo, the main city of Hokkaido.

TIME BAND

538	Buddhist religion introduced from China.
794	Permanent capital established at Kyoto.
1192	Rule by shoguns begins.
1543	First Europeans reach Japan.
1872	First railroad opened, linking Tokyo and Yokohama.
1894–5	Japan defeats China and acquires Taiwan.
1904–5	Japan defeats Russia.
1910	Japan takes over Korea.
1923	Earthquake destroys much of Tokyo and Yokohama.
1926–89	Reign of Emperor Hirohito.
1937	Japan tries to conquer China.
1941	Japan attacks U.S. naval base at Pearl Harbor.
1945	Atomic bombs dropped on Hiroshima and Nagasaki. Japan surrenders and loses overseas empire.
1946–52	Allied occupation of Japan.
1947	Japan adopts a democratic constitution.
1964	Olympic Games held in Tokyo.

Picture Pairs

Play Picture Pairs and see how many of the Japanese words in this book you actually remember! The instructions given here are for two to four players, but as your Japanese vocabulary increases, you might like to make more cards and include more players.

YOU WILL NEED:

OLD MAGAZINES

GIFT WRAP PAPER

METAL RULER

GLUE

STIFF PAPER

SCISSORS

THICK CARDBOARD

CUTTING MAT

PAINTS OR CRAYONS

PENCIL

CRAFT KNIFE

To make the cards

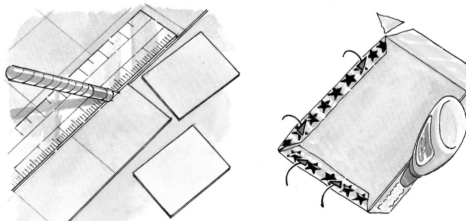

1. Draw 50 rectangles of the same size onto the cardboard and carefully cut them out using the craft knife.

2. Draw another 50 rectangles onto the wrapping paper and cut them out too. These rectangles should be about 1 inch (2 cm) longer and wider than the cardboard ones.

3. Cut the corners of the paper rectangles as shown and glue them onto your cards.

4. Draw 25 rectangles, slightly smaller than your cards, onto the stiff paper and cut them out.

5. Choose 25 Japanese words from this book and write them down with their English translations. (Keep this list beside you when you play the game.)

6. Look through the magazines and cut out any photographs that illustrate the words you have chosen. If you can't find suitable pictures, cut out some more rectangles from stiff paper and paint pictures of your words on them.

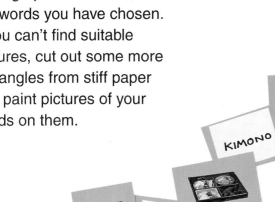

IKEBANA

SASHIMI

KIMONO

BENTO

HANA

7. Stick each photograph or picture onto the front of one of your cards. Glue the stiff paper rectangles onto the rest of the deck and write a Japanese word from your list on each one.

To play the game
The object of Picture Pairs is to collect pairs of cards made up of words and their matching picture.

Each player starts the game with seven cards. The rest of the deck is placed face-down on the table. If you have any pairs, put them on the table in front of you.

Then ask one of the other players if he/she has a card that you need to make a pair. If that player has the card requested, he/she must hand it over and you win the pair and have another turn. If he/she does not have the card, you take a card from the deck in the middle and the turn passes to the next person.

All word cards must be translated into English. If you cannot remember the translation of the word, look it up and miss your next turn.

The player who pairs all his/her cards first is the winner.

31

Index

Additional Photographs:
Bridgeman P.22; Bruce Coleman P.8; Hulton Deutsch P.29; Robert Harding P.14,15; Werner Forman P.23; Zefa P.8, P.18, P.22, P.23, P.29, Cover.